CUTEST ANIMALS...
THAT COULD KILL YOU!

DEADLY

PANDAS

Gareth Stevens
PUBLISHING

BY MARY MOLLY SHEA

Please visit our website, www.garethstevens.com. For a free color catalog of all our high-quality books, call toll free 1-800-542-2595 or fax 1-877-542-2596.

Cataloging-in-Publication Data

Names: Shea, Mary Molly.
Title: Deadly pandas / Mary Molly Shea.
Description: New York : Gareth Stevens Publishing, 2018. | Series: Cutest animals...that could kill you! | Includes index.
Identifiers: ISBN 9781538210802 (pbk.) | ISBN 9781538210826 (library bound) | ISBN 9781538210819 (6 pack)
Subjects: LCSH: Giant panda–Juvenile literature.
Classification: LCC QL737.C214 S524 2018 | DDC 599.789–dc23

First Edition

Published in 2018 by
Gareth Stevens Publishing
111 East 14th Street, Suite 349
New York, NY 10003

Copyright © 2018 Gareth Stevens Publishing

Designer: Sarah Liddell
Editor: Therese Shea

Photo credits: Cover, pp. 1, 15 Hung Chung Chih/Shutterstock.com; wood texture used throughout Imageman/Shutterstock.com; slash texture used throughout d1sk/Shutterstock.com; p. 4 basile20/Shutterstock.com; p. 5 Chendongshan/Shutterstock.com; p. 7 leungchopan/Shutterstock.com; pp. 8–9 Foreverhappy/Shutterstock.com; p. 11 JCREATION/Shutterstock.com; p. 13 Marcos del Mazo Valentin/Shutterstock.com; p. 17 ryoheim91/Shutterstock.com; p. 19 PHOTO BY LOLA/Shutterstock.com; p. 21 Katherine Feng/Minden Pictures/Minden Pictures/Getty Images.

Printed in China

CPSIA compliance information: Batch #CW18GS: For further information contact Gareth Stevens, New York, New York at 1-800-542-2595.

CONTENTS

n the glossary appear in **bold** type the first time they are used in the text.

Did you know that there are two kinds of animals called pandas? The giant panda is a type of bear, but the red panda isn't even **related** to it. Both are very cute!

In this book, you'll read about the animal that most think of when they hear the word "panda." Giant pandas have a special body and **behaviors** that help them in the wild. But sometimes, these **adaptations** make them dangerous, even to people. You'll learn that you shouldn't pet all cute animals—and never wild ones!

RED PANDA

BOTH THE RED PANDA
AND THE GIANT PANDA LIVE
ONLY IN CERTAIN PARTS
OF EAST ASIA.

GIANT PANDA

THE DANGEROUS DETAILS

Over the years, scientists have argued about whether giant pandas are bears, raccoons, or another kind of animal. Most now agree they're bears.

HOW GIANT?

Giant pandas are well known for their black-and-white fur. They have a round, white face with black fur around their eyes and round black ears. Their body is white, but their arms, legs, and shoulders are black.

How "giant" are giant panda bodies? Male pandas can be as long as 5 feet (1.5 m). That's not too big. But they can be very heavy—as much as 300 pounds (136 kg). That's more than a baby elephant! Female pandas are usually smaller.

THE DANGEROUS DETAILS

Scientists think the giant panda's black-and-white coloring may be a kind of **camouflage**!

GIANT PANDAS CAN
LIVE AS LONG AS 20 YEARS
IN THE WILD.

7

PANDAS IN THE TREES

You might see a giant panda in a zoo, but you won't see one in the wild unless you're in China. Giant pandas are found only in mountainous forests in central China. These forests are home to giant pandas' favorite food, a giant grass called bamboo.

Giant pandas have lived in forests for millions of years and have special adaptations that help them survive there. Thick fur keeps them warm in these cool, rainy places. They're also good climbers, though they don't look like it!

BABY PANDAS SPEND MORE TIME IN TREES THAN ADULT PANDAS DO. THIS HELPS KEEP THEM SAFE FROM ANIMALS THAT MIGHT HARM THEM.

BAMBOO BREAKFAST, LUNCH, AND DINNER

How much bamboo do giant pandas eat? Bamboo makes up almost 98 percent of everything a giant panda eats. This large grass doesn't have many **nutrients**, so the big creatures need to eat a lot of it. They may eat 40 pounds (18 kg) a day! Pandas get some water from bamboo, but they drink from rivers and other sources, too.

Giant pandas sometimes eat other kinds of plants, fish, rats, mice, and birds. However, bamboo is their favorite meal.

THE DANGEROUS DETAILS

To rid their body of bamboo waste, pandas may poop 50 times a day!

A PANDA'S DIET

98%
BAMBOO

2%
OTHER

PANDAS NEED TO LIVE
WHERE THERE IS MORE THAN
ONE KIND OF BAMBOO.
WHEN ONE KIND DIES OUT,
THEY'LL HAVE ANOTHER
KIND TO EAT.

A PANDA'S DAY

34%
OTHER

66%
FINDING AND
EATING FOOD

11

MUNCHING WITH MOLARS

Pandas have wide, flat teeth called molars in the back of their mouth. These teeth help them crush bamboo, which can be very tough.

A panda holds a bamboo stem with its five fingers. It has a special bone in its wrist that acts a bit like a thumb to help it hold on, too. Then, the panda uses its teeth to peel off the tough outer layers and uncover the soft parts inside the stem. Finally, it chows down!

THE DANGEROUS DETAILS

The long, sharp teeth in the front of a panda's mouth are called canines. They don't use them very much. They're the only bears that don't!

PANDAS EAT THE SHOOTS, LEAVES, AND STEMS OF BAMBOO.

13

SMELLY MESSAGES

Giant pandas aren't very friendly creatures. They usually like to be alone. This is one reason to stay away from pandas. However, some form groups of up to 15 bears in territories with a lot of bamboo. Different groups don't like to be near each other.

Scientists think pandas use smells to **communicate** with each other. They leave scents on trees and rocks around their territory. The scents can mean "leave me alone," "come join me," or "I'm looking for a **mate**."

THE DANGEROUS DETAILS

Male pandas may do handstands against trees to leave scent marks. The scent they leave comes from their rear end!

FEELING THREATENED

Giant pandas usually stay in their forests, away from places where people live. However, pandas have attacked people.

About 300 giant pandas live in zoos and special animal centers around the world. A few people have snuck into panda cages, often hoping to pet the cute creatures. Sometimes, pandas attacked the people. The bears most likely felt they were in danger. Though no one has been killed by pandas, people have been left with terrible wounds.

ALMOST ALL PANDAS IN ZOOS BELONG TO CHINA AND ARE "BORROWED" BY THE ZOOS.

THE DANGEROUS DETAILS

Giant pandas don't have any enemies in nature—except people!

STRONG JAWS

How can a cute bear that mostly eats grass its whole life hurt a person? Giant pandas have superpowerful **jaws**. In fact, scientists think the panda's head became bigger over many years to better fit its large jaws.

The giant panda's bite is one of the strongest of all animal bites. When a panda comes in contact with a person that it thinks might hurt it, it might bite the person, with horrible results. The bite can crush bamboo—and bone!

THE DANGEROUS DETAILS

The giant panda **evolved** its powerful bite to eat bamboo, but it may guard itself with its bite, too!

A GIANT PANDA'S
THROAT HAS A SPECIAL
LINING TO KEEP IT SAFE FROM
BAMBOO *SPLINTERS!*

19

A PANDA PROBLEM

Giant pandas once lived in more places than China. Hunting and the cutting down of forests drove them from all except some areas of China. China has begun guarding panda homes, but pandas aren't out of danger yet.

Scientists worry that **climate change** will kill many kinds of bamboo. Pandas only eat about 25 types. Different kinds bloom and die at different times. It can take years for the seeds to become full grown. Giant pandas may need your help in the future!

THE DANGEROUS DETAILS

Giant pandas have been **endangered** for years. Their population has grown to more than 1,800 bears in the wild.

SOME SCIENTISTS
TRACK PANDAS IN THE WILD
SO THEY CAN SEE HOW
PANDAS LIVE.

21

GLOSSARY

adaptation: a change in an animal that makes it better able to live in a place or situation

behavior: the way an animal acts, or behaves

camouflage: something such as color or shape that makes an animal hard to see

climate change: long-term change in Earth's climate, caused partly by human activities

communicate: to share thoughts or feelings about something by making sounds, moving, or acting a certain way

endangered: used to describe an animal or plant that has become very rare and that could die out completely

evolve: to change slowly, often into a better state

jaw: one of the two bones of the face where teeth grow

mate: one of two animals that come together to make babies

nutrient: matter that plants, animals, and people need to live and grow

related: in the same family

splinter: a thin, sharp piece of something that has broken off a larger piece

FOR MORE INFORMATION

BOOKS

Macleod, Steve. *Giant Panda.* New York, NY: Weigl Publishers, 2011.

Murray, Julie. *Giant Pandas.* Minneapolis, MN: ABDO, 2013.

Turnbull, Stephanie. *Panda.* Mankato, MN: Smart Apple Media, 2015.

WEBSITES

Giant Panda
kids.nationalgeographic.com/animals/giant-panda/
See some amazing photos of these animals.

Panda Watching
kids.sandiegozoo.org/animal-cams-videos/panda
Check out the "panda cam" at the San Diego Zoo!

INDEX